Sandmen

A Space Odyssey

Sandmen

A Space Odyssey

Diana Devlin & Irene Cunningham

A Poetry Conversation

First published 2019 by The Hedgehog Poetry Press,
5 Coppack House, Churchill Avenue, Clevedon. BS21 6QW

www.hedgehogpress.co.uk

Copyright © Diana Devlin & Irene Cunningham 2019. The right of Diana Devlin & Irene Cunningham to be identified as the authors of this work has been asserted in accordance with the Copyright, Designs and Patents Act 1988. All rights reserved. No part of this publication may be reproduced, stored in or introduced into a retrieval system, or transmitted in any form, or by any means (electronic, mechanical, photocopying, recording or otherwise) without prior written permissions of the publisher. Any person who does any unauthorised act in relation to this publication may be liable for criminal prosecution and civil claims for damages. All the characters in this publication are fictitious and any resemblance to real persons, living or dead, is purely coincidental.

ISBN: 978-1-9164806-4-3

Sandmen

A Space Odyssey

The first half of this poetic conversation offers the people's voice – how Hoi Polloi survive under a Tory government. The voices ramble into ridiculous scenarios concerning the fate of the planet Earth and its inhabitants. They switch to the sublime with musical meanderings as if even music would disappear...not transfer into a new world. Like any rollicking conversation, this ventures up alleyways and down theatrical stairs. Part call to arms, part wistful reverie dressed in disillusionment, this is a bizarre and at times alarming conversation born of the entangled dreams and nightmares of two quite different poets. All life is in here, from Morris dancers to urine sipping celebrities, dreamers to zombies, their strange tales told with affection and more than a touch of eccentricity.

Diana Devlin & Irene Cunningham, 2019

1

Keep your heads on –
they're coming
with their buckets of sand
and if you close your eyes
for one blinking second
they will bury your heads
in their sand –
your heads
in their buckets,
their buckets full
of your heads.
They're closing in on us all,
seeping into bone,
merging with marrow.
That gurgle in your veins
is the laughter of sandmen
settling in, bedding down.
They're coming
with their buckets of sand
and when they're done with you,
you won't see them shake
the sand out of their hair
and walk in the other direction.

2

My head
lies abed quite happy
in my cave
mostly because the air
wherever you are
is stuffed with shirts
hung on slovenly sitters
earning pay for loitering.
Scotland is a little fresher
than Westminster.
Tonight I close my windows
revel in silence;
there's a good view
from up here.
Geographically
we sit above them – will fill
their bloody buckets
with our shit. They're coming,
seeping in on the undercurrent
scuttling sideways
in the deep.

3

They think we're worms
they can make crawl and wriggle
under their crusty feet.

Earthworms don't need to fly –
they're winding clouds
in a well trodden sky –
but I need to fly.
All things neither soil nor sky,
all living things need to fly.

4

Noses stuck up, sniffing
the right to rule – funny how
they're never beautiful,
these ungainly folk.

They're ant-eaters; we laugh
at their skipping confidence.
Silly buggers think they're top
of our trees – squirrels.

They can fly anywhere
but neither universe nor gods
would grace them
with the lightness of being.

They're fossil fuel, with no souls.
It's said that angels sacrifice
free will, for their eternal
life, power, and position.

This lot will rule us into nothing,
and once we've gone
the planet will blow and cough
its lungs clear.

5

This flat blue space is all that's left of us,
the shape of memories baked hard as clay
under fading light of day. We

did this to ourselves, our world – and now
we watch from disembodied eyes afloat
in wistful distance, a trance too far.

The crystal lied, there was no happily ever after,
no time for sad farewells, no rolling credits
for this cast of carefree clowns. Just this –

a dog adrift among the stars, barking at the moon,
waiting for the tide to turn, in vain – we are
what we always were, no more.

6

They'll fill ships to go nowhere –
off this rock with our technology
and the best people...
Eeny meeny miny mo
venture forth a wagon-train.

Captains journaling as if
we'll matter in some distant future...
Valkyries riding the storm,
carried away in real life
fantasy orchestrating
human existence elsewhere.

All life is here and all we've got.
Do I care if we've overlooked
some universal truth
in our race towards oblivion? I think
not. A cave dweller won't lose sleep over my choice
of shoes, whether I choose to walk in them or
dance to death's door. And when I go to sleep
my choice of bed is mine, my choice,
my bed, this music in my head,
my head,
my very human head.

If and when they go they'll be
so distant from history and old ways
that clog dancing and Morris
clacking bell-ringing
won't be chosen...or the kilt
with its sword-dancing.

Fresh starts in untamed land
is a serious business
until stills and giggle-juice are up
and running, flutes whittled...
space-digeridoos for evening
settlement under shatterproof domes.

We're a long way from home, waiting
for a lift that'll never come, pining for a past
that has forgotten us and lurks in the dreams
of strangers embedded in our flesh
like shrapnel. Sometimes,
on a clear night, we see their ghostly forms
moving below our skin.
In the stillness
we feel their matchstick fingers
snapping, hear their tiny voices
calling us out. Their truth
tingles on our tongues.
It leaves us numb.

7

There was a man
entangled in my nights; he filled me
with music, made me a slave,
robbed my mind, emptied
all my vessels. Now
nothing penetrates.

What have I missed
in my casual dismissal of pain...
expecting everyone
to brush battle off?
If it doesn't kill you
get up and kick something.
My eyes are reversed telescopes,
holding me to myself.

Some of me is missing.

8

Life grates. I've lost shavings of me
along the way. Rasped remains reach out
on a quest for reconstruction, wholeness –
but the picture wanes and fades
despite the desperate layering of experience,
the clogging dust of time.
We are but malicious indifference:
all life is loss we build ourselves.

9

You sound zombiefied,
captured, forced to drink your own pee –
it can't be that bad if you aren't drowned
yet...or are you blootered?
Don't be thinking about loch-swimming
though maybe you'll be
empty enough to begin again.

The new you might jump a train,
grab divine guidance
from promotions with fancies
and cravings: instant body-re-shaping,
sudden cash deposits flood
your accounts – the future could be
magicked. You'd be free.
Malice was a mad old bitch
from Clydebank.

10

If it's good enough for Madonna, it'll do for me –
I'm not too proud to sup the amber nectar,
freshly squeezed. You should try it,
all that coffee's bad for you but a goblet
of your own urine sets you back on track.
I heard an old track today, it set my head a-spin
– now I've got Rod Stewart
skating through my brain like a hedgehog
on speed. You, my friend,
are a bad influence.

11

Really, it's these men
and their songs that drag
us off the straight n narrow.
I had George Michael the other week,
that husky whisper asking me
to go outside...and I was up for it
all right but, it wasn't the time
for ghostly shenanigans.
I just sighed, finished making
the bed. But it sparked something,
you know? I forgot
what the song was about and really
felt like going outside
my every day stuff.
Well, my old heart was lifted.

Have you ever
had to seduce a man?
I offered my young self
to the hotel night porter
so we could eat; he had keys
to the kitchen. We had a wall
full of cookbook pages,
a promised wage at the end of the week –
our cash was spent on beer
and fags, and train fare, to suffer
a decrepit mansion, staff quarters,
fed shrivened meals, starved,
danced with Leo Sayer
and Neil Sedaka.
Music is enough.

12

I've been stuffed full of shenanigans in my time,
in another world, in different skin, almost
not me ... ach ...
as for music being enough, it followed me – still does –
like a cloud that bursts on a whim
and soaks the bones of me until I'm so damp with it
I can't speak. Funny how I never liked
the tunes from my own era, always had a hankering
for the exotic... couldn't live without music.
It's the soft skin of the stone in me.

13

I fell in love last night.
A movie played a song at the end,
carried me away onto Amazon –
I bought two wee words
Ordinary Human.
My hair was waving!

You could
blame music for bad choices
in men, and
quantities of alcohol.
Often, I've no idea what songs
are about...I get all bent with the tune –
my mother should've named me Melody.
How can two words and a husky voice
melt a woman of my size?

In these new generations
everyone's genetically altered –
how could they not be
when consuming numbers?
It's the dance of survival;
everything's recycled...
even the dead are measured weight,
food, material, replacement parts.
Every ounce used – fat rendered
for soap to keep wheels turning.

14

I dream myself beautiful, reclining
in a Venetian gondola, as a drowsy crimson sun
settles on my thighs like a cat.

Under the Rialto bridge the sun steals the upper hand
on sudden shade and my eyelids are invaded by tigers.
In the early evening air warm skin tingles cool.

You think you're in love but you haven't seen
the Grand Canal, felt it chuckle like a child
as the tickle of the vaporetto vibrates along its flanks.

What will become of this, the city of my dreams,
once they've purged our planet, modified
the genetics of life itself, packed us off for good?

There's no return for zombies, new prisons
will replace my Bridge of Sighs and rivers
will flow back to anonymity. We

did this to ourselves, our world – and now
we watch from disembodied hearts afloat
in wistful distance, a trance too far.

Diana Devlin

Diana Devlin is a Scottish-Italian poet who has worked as a translator, lexicographer and teacher and now writes full time. Her poetry has been widely published online, in anthologies and in print. She runs a writing group in Dumbarton and is working on her first collection. When she is not writing, she spends her time reading or working in her art journal, although the only thing she has in common with Picasso is the shape of her nose. Her home near Loch Lomond is full of music, books and cats, just how she likes it.

Irene Cunningham

Irene Cunningham has had many poems published in lit mags, including *London Review of Books* (as Maggie York), *New Welsh Review, New Writing Scotland, Stand, Iron, Writing Women, Northwords Now, Poetry Scotland* and others. Recent publications: *Picaroon, South Bank Poetry, I am not a Silent Poet, Riggwelter The Lake, Shoreline of Infinity, Blue Nib* and *Laldy!* She has published three collections of poetry, available at Amazon. She lives at Loch Lomond, is passionate for art and photography and is a constant digital doodler. One of her poems published this year has been nominated for The Pushcart Prize.
http://ireneintheworld.wixsite.com/writer

www.ingramcontent.com/pod-product-compliance
Lightning Source LLC
Chambersburg PA
CBHW021135080526
44587CB00012B/1302